FARM ANIMALS
DUCK

Katie Dicker

A[+]

Smart Apple Media

Published by Smart Apple Media,
an imprint of Black Rabbit Books
P.O. Box 3263, Mankato, Minnesota, 56002
www.blackrabbitbooks.com

Printed in the United States of America,
at Corporate Graphics in North Mankato, Minnesota.

Designed by Hel James
Edited by Mary-Jane Wilkins

Library of Congress Cataloging-in-Publication Data

Dicker, Katie.
 Duck / Katie Dicker.
    p. cm. -- (Farm animals)
 Includes bibliographical references and index.
 ISBN 978-1-62588-020-8
 1. Ducks--Juvenile literature. I. Title.
 SF505.3.D525 2014
 636.5'97--dc23

                         2013000058

Photo acknowledgements
l = left, r = right, t = top, b = bottom
title page Eric Isselee/Shutterstock; page 3, 4, 5, 6
iStockphoto/Thinkstock; 7 BGSmith/Shutterstock;
8 iStockphoto/Thinkstock; 9 Hemera/Thinkstock,
10 iStockphoto/Thinkstock, 11 Daniel Alvarez/Shutterstock;
12 iStockphoto/Thinkstock; 14 Mazzzur/Shutterstock;
15 Hemera/Thinkstock; 16 Goodluz/Shutterstock;
17 Zoonar/Thinkstock; 18 Ekkachai/Shutterstock;
19 Wild Arctic Pictures/Shutterstock; 20 iStockphoto/
Thinkstock; 21 iStockphoto/Thinkstock, r Eric Isselee/
Shutterstock; 22 iStockphoto/Thinkstock; 23 Heidi
Robberts/Shutterstock
Cover nbiebach/Shutterstock

DAD0507
052013
9 8 7 6 5 4 3 2 1

Contents

Quack!

My World

I am a duck.
I live on a farm with
lots of other ducks.

4

Here are some of my flock.
We like to live outside. Whenever we can,
we splash and paddle in pools of water.

At night, ducks need a shelter
to stay safe from animals
such as foxes and owls.

5

Head to Foot

Our feathers keep us warm and dry.
They have an oil coating to make them waterproof.

Ducks can swim very fast. They use their webbed feet like paddles.

Our webbed feet help us to swim. They also make us waddle when we walk!

A duck has soft, fluffy feathers close to its body for extra warmth.

Keeping Clean

I clean my feathers with my beak. This is called preening. I can turn my head to reach all parts of my body.

Preening also keeps
my feathers waterproof.
As I move my beak, the oil
spreads around my body.

**A duck dips its
head into water
to clean its eyes
and nostrils.**

Time to Eat

We like to eat plants, seeds, insects, and worms. The farmer also gives us grain.

My mouth is called a beak or a bill. It helps me to grab and grip my food.

Peck

10

These ducks are dabblers. They put their heads under water to search for food.

Ducks also need plenty of clean, fresh drinking water.

Laying Eggs

Ducks sit on their eggs to keep them warm. After about 28 days, the ducklings are ready to hatch.

Female ducks lay an egg every morning. They make a nest of soft hay and line it with feathers.

Male ducks are called drakes. A drake is needed to breed baby ducklings. Each duckling grows inside a female duck's egg.

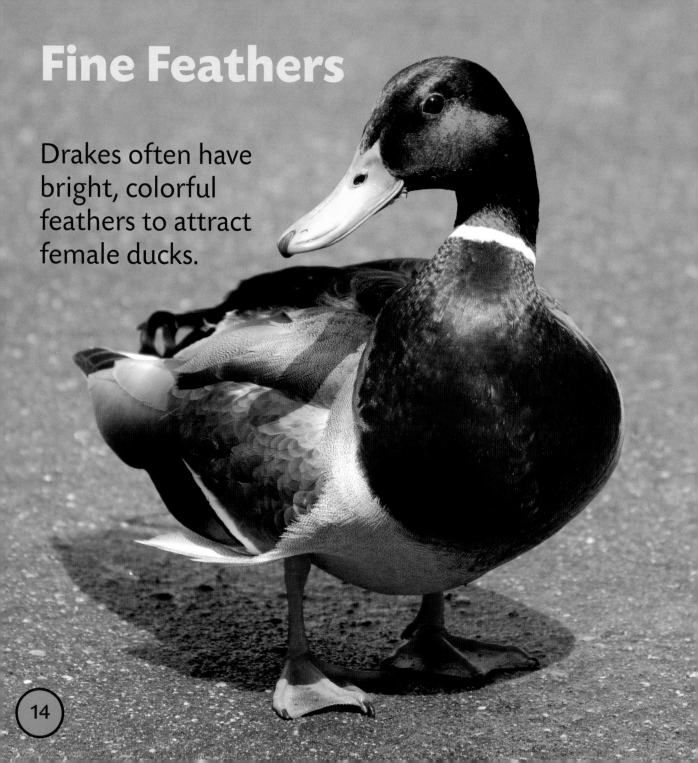

Fine Feathers

Drakes often have bright, colorful feathers to attract female ducks.

The feathers of female ducks are colored
to suit their surroundings. These colors
help them to hide from predators.

Female ducks quack,
but drakes make a
soft, muffled sound.

Who Looks After Us?

The farmer gives us fresh straw and hay to keep our shelter clean and dry.

A visit from the vet also helps to keep us healthy.

The farmer checks that we have clean water to drink, and collects our eggs every day.

Farm Produce

Ducks are farmed for their meat and eggs, and for their soft feathers, called down.

Duck eggs are larger than chicken eggs, with a harder shell and a large yolk.

The eider duck has very soft feathers. These feathers are used to make quilts, pillows, and duvets.

Quilts made from eider duck feathers are called eiderdowns.

Ducks Around the World

Farmers in countries all over the world keep ducks. Some ducks live in the wild and others are kept as pets. Here are some of the different breeds.

White Crested, Holland

Mandarin, Asia

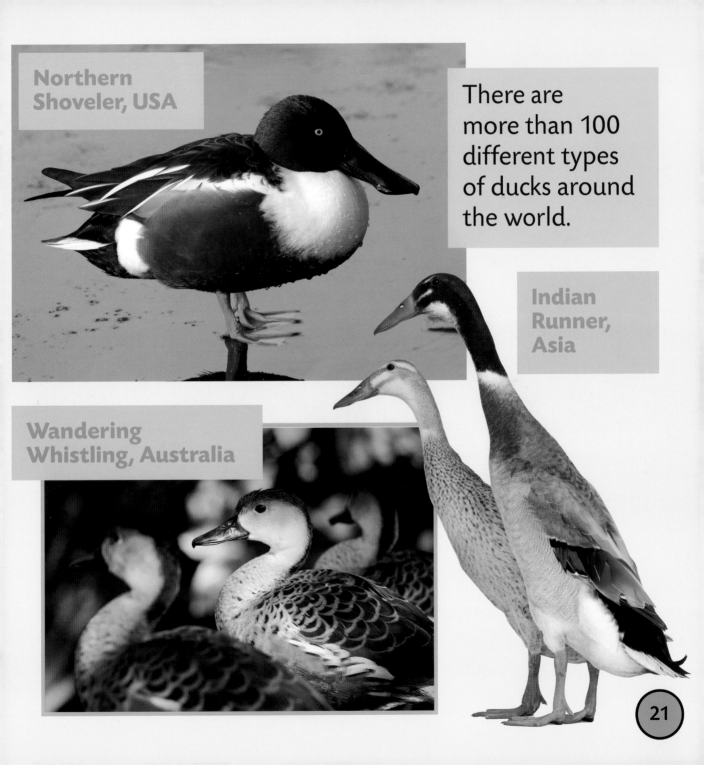

Northern Shoveler, USA

There are more than 100 different types of ducks around the world.

Indian Runner, Asia

Wandering Whistling, Australia

21

Did You Know?

Ducks live for between two and fifteen years, depending on the type.

Ducks cannot feel the cold in their feet, even when they swim in icy water!

Ducks sometimes sleep with one eye open, to keep watch for predators.

Ducks are good at standing on one leg without falling over.

Useful Words

breed
A male and female duck breed to make ducklings.

flock
A group of animals that live together.

hatch
A baby duck hatches when it comes out of its egg.

nostrils
The holes in a duck's beak that it uses to breathe.

predators
Animals that hunt other animals for food.

Index

Web Links

www.animalcorner.co.uk/farm/ducks/duck_about.html

www.kiddyhouse.com/Farm/ducks.html

www.kidskonnect.com/subject-index/13-animals/438-ducks.html

www.facts-about.org.uk/facts-about-duck.htm